Forest Fires

Forest Fires

Lisa Trumbauer

Franklin Watts
A Division of Scholastic Inc.
New York • Toronto • London • Auckland • Sydney
Mexico City • New Delhi • Hong Kong
Danbury, Connecticut

For my brother, Steven Trutkoff

Note to readers: Definitions for words in **bold** can be found in the Glossary at the back of this book.

Photographs © 2005: AP/Wide World Photos: 45 (Thomas Cordova/Inland Valley Daily Bulletin), cover (Helen Richardson Denver Post), 39; Corbis Images: 24 (Patrick Bennett), 36, 37 (Bettmann), 2 (Jonathan Blair), 17 (J. Emilio Flores), 26 top (Laurence Fordyce/Eye Ubiquitous), 16, 18, 19 bottom, 21 (Raymond Gehman), 48 (Fred Greaves), 23 (Mark A. Johnson), 19 top, 20, 28, 32 (Reuters), 30, 47 (Galen Rowell), 6 (Royalty-Free), 5 top, 12 (Tom Stewart), 29 (Michael S. Yamashita), 11 (Jim Zuckerman), 34; Dembinsky Photo Assoc.: 5 bottom, 26 bottom (Patti McConville), 42 (John Mielcarek), 46 (Jean & Ted Reuther); Getty Images: 40 (Stephen Ferry), 38 (Hulton Archive), 22 (Spike Mafford/The Image Bank); National Geographic Image Collection: 8 (Michael S. Quinton), 14, 15 (Rich Reid), 10 (Joel Sartore); Superstock, Inc./The Millennium Photo Project: 6; The Image Works/Jack Kurtz: 33.

Illustration page 9 by Bob Italiano

The photograph on the cover shows wildfires near Deckers, Colorado. The photograph opposite the title page shows forest fires in Yellowstone National Park in Wyoming.

Library of Congress Cataloging-in-Publication Data

Trumbauer, Lisa, 1963–
 Forest fires / Lisa Trumbauer.
      p. cm. — (Watts library)
 Includes bibliographical references and index.
 ISBN 0-531-12284-0
 1. Forest fires—Juvenile literature. 2. Forest fires—United States—Juvenile literature.
I. Title. II. Series.
 SD421.23.T78 2005
  634.9'618—dc22   2005000915

Contents

As dry trees and vegetation catch fire, this forest fills with flames. It will take teams of experienced firefighters to control this blaze.

Chapter One

Fire's Components

The summer of 1988 in Yellowstone National Park was dry. Hardly any rain had fallen during the month of June, and small ponds, marshes, and streams began to dry up. The grasslands turned from green to brown. Storm clouds came, but they brought only lightning, not rain. The lightning started many fires in Yellowstone that summer, but the real fire had yet to ignite.

The blaze that would eventually take over Yellowstone was ignited not by lightning but by people. Woodcutters in neighboring Targhee National Forest started a fire by accident, and it soon spread into Yellowstone. Firefighters now had several fires to battle, but no matter how hard they worked, the flames kept growing and spreading. It would take three months—and the burning of more than 1 million acres (405,000 hectares)—before the fires in Yellowstone were finally extinguished.

Smoke drifts among charred tree trunks as flames glow behind during the Yellowstone fires of 1988.

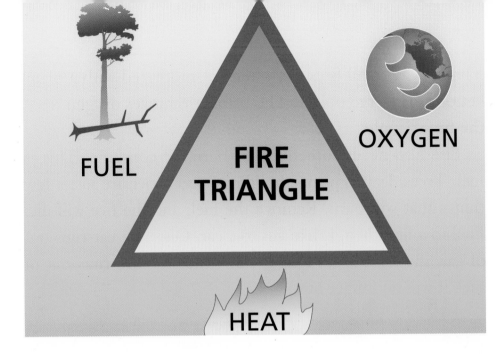

A diagram of the fire triangle shows the three components of fire.

To understand **forest fires,** you need to know how a fire starts. After you know what is necessary for a fire to begin, then you can explore the characteristics of fire, learn how people battle fires, find out about historic fires, and discover how fires can actually improve the **ecology** of a forest.

How Does Fire Start?

In order for a fire to ignite, there must be three things—oxygen, fuel, and heat. These components together are called the **fire triangle.** Take away one side of a triangle, and the triangle collapses. The same applies with fire. Take away one component necessary for fire to start, and the fire goes out. Let's look at the components in more detail.

Oxygen is in the air. We need oxygen to live, and fire does, too. The air we breathe is 21 percent oxygen. Fire needs only 16 percent oxygen. Without oxygen, fire will die.

A Long History

For thousands of years, humans have used fire to clear land, reduce the threat of wildfire to their homes and communities, and provide fuel to cook food, boil water, and keep warm.

9

In Our Solar System

Of all the planets in our solar system, only Earth has the three components necessary to make fire: oxygen, fuel, and heat (from lightning).

That is why small fires can often be smothered with a blanket or other large object. The blanket removes oxygen from the fire triangle.

Fire also needs something to burn, or consume. This is fuel. Trees, leaves, plants, buildings, and paper are just a few things that will burn. Remove the fuel, and the fire will die. Fuel to a fire, then, is like gas to a car. Once the car runs out of gas, the car will no longer run. Once the fire runs out of fuel, it will no longer burn.

The fuel in this fire is driftwood. When the fuel is used up, the campfire will die out.

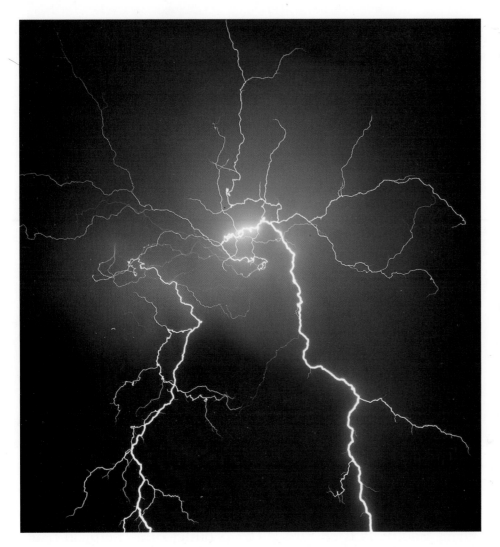

Naturally caused forest fires are most often sparked by lightning. The fuels, which must be dry, are typically wood, leaves, or grass.

Did You Know?

Flammable means "able to burn." The word *inflammable* means the same thing!

The third thing fire needs is heat. The temperature must be extremely high for a fire to begin. For example, wood burns at 617 degrees Fahrenheit (325 degrees Celsius). That's 405 degrees Fahrenheit more than the temperature at which water boils. Lightning can be as hot as 50,000° F (28,000° C). That's five times hotter than the sun! With so much heat, no wonder lightning can start fires in a forest.

This campfire is the result of a chemical reaction that requires heat, oxygen, and fuel from the heated wood.

What Is Fire?

Once these three components are in place, a fire can start. But what, exactly, is fire? Fire is the product of a chemical reaction. It is the energy that is released when (1) the temperature is hot enough, (2) the air has at least 16 percent oxygen, and (3) fuel is available. When oxygen combines with the fuel, or **combustible** material, and the temperature is high, then energy is released in the form of fire.

You may be familiar with small fires. For example, light a match, and you've created a small flame. Turn on a gas stove, and blue-orange flames sprout up under your pot. Stack wood and some newspaper in a fireplace, click a lighter next to it, and watch the fire burn.

But did you know that what is burning is not really the wood in the fireplace but a gas? As the fuel heats up, it is changed, or converted, to a gas. The gas given off by the heated wood rises a tiny bit, allowing for more oxygen than is available on the surface of the wood. Now you've got heat, oxygen, and fuel in the form of gas (from the heated log). You've got fire!

A **fireball** is a perfect example of this gas in play. A fireball is a burst of fire that may occur several feet above a burning tree. The gas emitted by the burning tree has risen above the tree, and the gas bursts into flames when it has sufficient oxygen and a spark to ignite it. The tree isn't burning—the gas given off by the tree is burning.

When Fire Is Wild

Fire that is burning completely out of control on open land is called a **wildfire.** Wildfires move very quickly, sometimes up to 15 miles (24 kilometers) an hour. It is very difficult for people and even many animals to outrun a wildfire.

Wildfires can seem to take on a life and personality all their own. They breathe and eat, consuming everything in their path. Fires that burn out of control can grow and change direction, moving where the wind and fuel take them. Controlling them can be a dangerous challenge.

Not Flammable

Not all things can burn. Stone and metal, for example, are not flammable.

13

This forest fire started in Santa Barbara, California. Strong offshore Santa Ana winds helped spread the damaging fire.

Chapter Two

Meet the Fires

Imagine hiking in the woods with your friends. You stop to make a little fire to cook your picnic lunch. After eating your last marshmallow, you throw water on the smoldering remains of your fire. You and your friends set off for an afternoon of hiking, your campfire forgotten. Soon wind blows a little air on the fire's embers. Some leaves blow by, and the dry vegetation sparks to life. A fire has just been reborn.

Each year in the United States, about

A neglected campfire started this wildfire at Point Reyes National Seashore in Marin County, California. The 1995 fire burned thousands of acres.

Location

Forest fires in the northeastern United States are much more likely to be started by people than in Alaska and the Rocky Mountains, where lightning is more likely to be the culprit.

100,000 forest fires burn. Do you think more fires are started by lightning or by people? The answer is—by people! Only 10 percent of all forest fires are started by lightning. That means 90 percent of all forest fires are started by people.

Of course, most people do not start fires intentionally. A campfire that was not totally extinguished may leave behind a few sparks. A cigarette butt tossed on a rocky hiking trail could leave a trail of sparks as it is thrown. Glass lying in the sun can cause leaves to burn as the sun shines through the glass. If the temperature of the air is warm enough and the trees and plants are dry enough, seemingly unimportant actions can bring about a forest fire.

Types of Fires

Fires come in three forms. There are **surface fires, crown fires,** and **ground fires.**

Most of the forest fires in the United States are surface fires. These types of fires burn only the surface of the forest, below the treetops. They consume leaves, sticks, trees that have toppled over, hollow logs, and other vegetation close to the ground. In surface fires, trees that are alive and standing are not usually consumed.

When a fire does start to burn the tops of trees, it has become a crown fire. During a surface fire, the fire spreads along the ground. But during a crown fire, the fire can leap

A tree surrounded by wildflowers and verdant brush goes up in flames. This wildfire is a crown fire.

A ground fire burns below the ground's surface. It spreads by burning dead plant material such as dry leaves and pine needles.

from treetop to treetop, usually driven by the wind. During a crown fire, you might see a fireball exploding over the top of a tree.

The third type of fire is a ground fire. Here, the fire burns within the ground, feeding on decayed matter that lies below the surface. Some ground fires burn the dead roots of trees and other plants. Ground fires may sometimes appear to have gone out, and then they show up again several feet away. They can travel underground slowly, burning their way from root to decaying matter.

Fire Characteristics

If you happen to see a **wildland fire** blazing on TV, you might be able to identify some of its characteristics. For example, a fire might appear to have long arms that reach up into the sky. These arms are actually called the **fingers of flame.** The **flaming front** is that part of the fire that burns most rapidly. This part of the fire is usually moving forward. The fire behind the flaming front is mainly smoldering.

Fires usually move to where new fuel can be found. It would not make sense for a fire to turn around and move backward, for it has already burned the fuel behind it. Fires also move in the direction that the wind is blowing. Wind provides new oxygen for the fire, making fires burn more strongly. The **flanks of a fire** are the parts of the fire that are roughly parallel to the direction in which the fire is spreading.

The **head of a fire** is that part of the fire that moves fastest. The fire moves slowest at the back and at intermediate speeds on the flanks. A head fire is often the most intense and

Fire races up the trees in this forest fire (top).

The fastest part of a wildfire is the head of the fire (bottom).

dangerous kind of fire. A fire is said to be a **running fire** if it is spreading very quickly and its head is easy to see.

Sometimes the sparks from a forest fire can set off fires nearby. These fires are called **spot fires.** Fires can also have **flare-ups**—a sudden quickening or strengthening of the fire. Flare-ups don't last very long, and they do not drastically change how firefighters control a blaze.

Fire flares up a ridge as firefighters look on during a forest fire at California's Sequoia National Forest.

Blowups, on the other hand, can lead to major changes in plans. Blowups are bigger than flare-ups, and they spread more quickly and have more intensity. Therefore, blowups are harder to control.

Blowups can lead to **firestorms,** which have very destructive **indrafts** (strong winds drawn into a fire by a column of rising air heated by the fire). Some indrafts can lead to **fire whirls**—tornado-like funnels of hot air and gases. The fire whirl rises in the air and carries with it not only flames, but

Firestorms are fires of extreme intensity. A firestorm fans its own flames by creating its own draft.

21

A brush fire burns land covered mostly with low-lying plants. This brush fire tears through dry scrub vegetation in the hills outside Guanajuato, Mexico.

smoke and debris, which can cause spot fires. A fire whirl may be as small as 2 feet (61 centimeters) or as large as 500 feet (153 meters) in diameter.

Fire Sizes

Not all wildland fires are classified as large—meaning fierce enough to cause concern and harm to wildlife, people, and property. For example, a **creeping fire** has a low flame and does not spread very fast. A **brush fire** mainly burns plants low to the ground, like shrubs. A **grass fire** burns on prairies and fields. And a **smoldering fire** burns in the ground with

What's a Hot Spot?

A hot spot is a part of a fire that is extremely active.

smoke but without flames and is barely spreading. Under certain conditions, any of these fires can grow into large fires.

Firefighters have specific requirements for classifying fires. They consider the area of the land affected and the fire's behavior based on weather conditions and its potential to spread. A **project fire** is an especially large fire. It is so large that organizations with more resources than a local fire department are called in to help contain it.

Grass-fire season is usually spring and summer, when prairies and fields are most dry.

Rangers monitor the status of local, state, and national parks and forests. This ranger works at Daniel Boone National Forest in eastern Kentucky.

Chapter Three

Battling the Blazes

Our first line of defense against wildfires is prevention. Rangers, who monitor and care for local, state, and national forests and parks, routinely check their land for any sign that a wildland fire might erupt. Planes may fly overhead, looking for any smoke or fire potential. Sometimes the planes have infrared cameras to detect heat.

When a fire is spotted, rangers must decide if they should allow the fire to continue burning or take action to put it out. Because fire can have positive effects,

History's Longest-Running Service Campaign

The Smokey Bear campaign was created in 1944. The forest ranger character named Smokey Bear cautioned children and adults alike, "Only *you* can prevent forest fires!" As part of an effort to address the increasing number of wildfires on U.S. wildlands, officials replaced *forest fires* with the word *wildfires* in 2001.

From a fire watch tower, members of a fire crew can observe local weather conditions and assess any dangers resulting from a change in fire behavior or weather.

Some Outdoor Safety Tips from Smokey Bear

- Know your county's outdoor burning regulations. Unlawful trash burning is a punishable offense.
- Don't park vehicles on dry grass.
- Inspect your campsite before leaving.
- Leave your campsite as natural as possible, traveling on trails and other durable surfaces.
- Never take burning sticks out of a fire.
- Store flammable liquid containers in a safe place.
- Keep stoves, lanterns, and heaters away from combustibles.
- Never use stoves, lanterns, and heaters inside a tent.
- Never take any type of fireworks on public lands.
- At the first sign of a wildfire, leave area immediately by established trails or roads. Contact a ranger as soon as possible. If escape route is blocked, go to the nearest lake or stream.

the rangers sometimes just monitor the burning fire. But if the rangers think the fire has the potential to spread quickly and harm people, homes, or businesses, they prepare to take action.

Calling in the Crews

If you've ever seen a forest fire on television, you've probably also seen interviews with men and women, dirty and exhausted from fighting the fire but determined to keep working. Firefighters specially trained to deal with the hottest part of a forest fire are called **hotshots.**

People interested in becoming hotshots apply to one of several government agencies, including the U.S. Forest Service, the Bureau of Land Management, and the National Park Service. Some Native American groups also run their own

A hotshot crew patrols the Angeles National Forest in search of hotspots after a wildfire scorched several thousand acres near Santa Clarita, California, in 2002.

hotshot programs. Applicants who meet the requirements and complete their training then become members of a firefighting crew, which usually has about twenty men and women.

All firefighting crews must be available twenty-four hours a day, seven days a week during the fire season. The fire season is the months during which wildland fires most often occur because of warmer temperatures, less rainfall, and the sun's heat. For the western United States, fire season runs from May through October.

When a fire breaks out, crews may be called in from around the country. When called into action, a truck, van, or plane takes them as close to the fire as possible. Then they must hike through the forest, with all their gear, until they reach the fire.

Hotshot crews typically work twelve-hour shifts. Eighty-hour weeks are not uncommon during the fire season. Living conditions can be tough. Hotshots often have to sleep on the ground, and it may be several days before they can get a shower. The work of a hotshot is not only dangerous, but physically, mentally, and emotionally exhausting.

The Smoke Jumpers

More than sixty years ago, a new breed of forest firefighter was introduced at a blaze in Idaho's Nez Perce National Forest. On July 12, 1940, firefighters wearing parachutes jumped from airplanes, landing as close to the fire as possible. These new firefighters were called **smoke jumpers.**

Since then, smoke jumpers have played a critical role in controlling and putting out forest fires in the West. Hotshots might not be able to reach a fire for several hours, or even days, as they hike through a forest. Smoke jumpers can place themselves almost immediately right in the middle of the action.

A smoke-jumping crew usually includes sixteen people. A pilot and copilot fly the airplane. Another member of the crew serves as the spotter—

Students training to be smoke jumpers wait inside an airplane to take a practice jump near Missoula, Montana.

29

the person who identifies a good place for the smoke jumpers to land. The remaining crew members then jump from the airplane, usually two at a time.

How to Fight Fires

If you had a small fire in your house, how might you put it out? You would probably throw water on it or douse it with the contents of a fire extinguisher. Firefighters try to do the same by putting out the fire with chemicals, dirt, or water.

To extinguish a fire, you have to remove one part of the fire triangle—oxygen, fuel, or heat. Chemicals and water eliminate two parts of the fire triangle—heat and oxygen. The water or chemicals can cool down the fire, while at the same time smothering the fire and depriving it of oxygen.

A bomber drops chemicals to help extinguish a wildland fire.

For a small fire at home, you have an easy water source. Turn on the kitchen faucet and put out the fire. But what would you do in the middle of the forest? Where would you hook up your hose or fill your buckets of water? How could you get high enough to put out the fire in a tall tree?

The answer is with aircraft. Firefighters use airplanes to release chemicals directly on top of the fire. Or if a lake or river is nearby, crews can use helicopters to scoop up water with buckets. Then they can fly above the fire and dump the water to help extinguish the flames.

Another way to control fire is to remove its fuel. Wildland firefighters do this by getting ahead of the fire. They will cut down trees—perhaps even burn the trees—to remove the fuel the fire needs. This strategy is called building a **fire line.** **Burning out** is another way to burn away fuels ahead of a fire. Fires are set along the inner edge of a fire line. These fires are less intense and move much more slowly than head fires.

Tools of the Trade

Typical firefighters rely almost solely on water to smother and cool fires. But wildland fires are often so large and so hot that water alone is not an option. For large project fires, firefighters need special tools to work through the trees and vegetation. The tools must be lightweight and versatile. Forest firefighters don't have a truck or a station nearby to supply them with more gear. They must be able to carry their tools with them.

Heroes in Helicopters

The U.S. Forest Service has five hundred helicopters available to fight forest fires. Helicopters were first used to fight fires in southern California in 1947. Loaded with water and fire-retardant chemicals, helicopters transport crews to battle a blaze. A helicopter's firefighters are members of **helitack crews.** Unlike airplanes, helicopters can hover over firefighters on the ground and lift them to safety.

Here are some firefighting tools and how they are used:

Ax: Firefighters use axes to chop down trees and clear debris in their path.

Backpack water pump: This piece of equipment is for use during the initial attack on small fires and for mopping up smoldering ground fires.

Chainsaw: This tool helps firefighters cut down burning **snags** or remove logs after snags have fallen.

Drip torch: It may seem odd for a firefighter to carry a torch, but a drip torch allows firefighters to burn out fuels along a fire line.

McLeod: Firefighters use this combination rake and hoe to cut through and clear away vegetation.

Pulaski: This dual-purpose tool can chop down trees with its ax side and dig with the other side. A forest ranger named Ed Pulaski invented this tool in 1910.

Shovel: Firefighting shovels are light enough to be easily carried. They have a sharp edge to cut down small trees. Shovels can be used to scrape away flammable materials from the ground during the building of fire lines and to throw dirt on a fire to smother it.

With each wildland fire, firefighters can learn something new. They may learn a new way to halt the blaze or to get it under control. They may learn which techniques and tools are better for handling different types of fires. They may also learn about themselves and their crewmates as they battle the fires.

In the Thick of It

What happens if a firefighter is caught in the middle of a fire? All firefighters must carry a fire-proof shelter. A firefighter about to be engulfed in a fire would unfold the shelter and jump inside. The inside of the shelter may get hot—about 200° F (93° C)—but it might save the firefighter's life.

Men stand and look at the ruins of buildings after the Great Chicago Fire of 1871.

Chapter Four

Some Famous Fires

During the Yellowstone fires of 1988, much wildland was burned, but thankfully, no human lives were lost. Even though it took weeks to control and end the fire, it was by no means the worst blaze in the history of the United States. Several other famous fires top the list. Each one leads to new knowledge about fires and how to prevent, detect, and fight them.

This illustration shows the chaotic scene of people trying to flee the Great Peshtigo Fire of 1871.

Fires of the 1800s

One of the worst fires on record occurred not in the West, as many forest fires do today, but in the East. The year was 1825, and the northeastern part of the North American continent was experiencing a drought. Lumbermen in the area had set a fire, which raged out of control. When it was all over, 160 people lost their lives. About 3 million acres (1.2 million ha) throughout Maine and New Brunswick, Canada, were destroyed. That's twice as many acres lost as the Yellowstone fires of 1988.

In 1871, a fire ignited in the Midwest, in Wisconsin near the Michigan border. The weather that summer had been extremely hot and dry. Local people often intentionally burned trees that had been cut down to clear land for farming.

Also back then, sparks from steam train engines could quickly ignite dry grass. These factors, along with a dry wind blowing up from the southwest, contributed to the Peshtigo fire, which began on October 8. The Great Peshtigo Fire of 1871 might not have burned the most land—about 1 million acres (405,000 ha)—but it took the most lives—about 1,300 people. Many historians consider it to be the most tragic fire in U.S. history.

The Great Chicago Fire of 1871

At about the same time the Peshtigo fire was creating havoc in northeastern Wisconsin, a fire was raging in Chicago. In fact, more people probably remember the Chicago fire of 1871 than the Peshtigo fire. The same weather conditions that plagued the Wisconsin town also plagued Chicago—a dry, hot summer, plenty of wood, an errant spark, and a southwesterly wind that fanned the flames.

Although tens of thousands of buildings were destroyed, around 300 people were killed, and 100,000 were left homeless, only about 2,000 acres (810 ha) burned. The Great Chicago Fire is not included on "worst fire" lists.

In this photograph from about 1910, structural firefighters work on a tall building. Structural firefighters fight fires that start in and burn any building, shelter, or other structure.

Fires of the Early 1900s

One of the most devastating fires in the United States occurred in 1910. Often called the Big Blowup, the fires that engulfed western portions of Washington, Idaho, and Montana burned through about 3 million acres (1.2 million ha) of forests. Entire towns went up in flames. Eighty-five people perished, more than seventy of whom were firefighters.

The fires lasted for only two days—August 20 and 21. They were able to spread very quickly because of hurricane-force winds, which are winds exceeding 74 miles (119 km) per hour. Reports claim that the fire's smoke could be seen by ships in the Pacific Ocean, 500 miles (805 km) off the west coast of North America and as far east as New York State. About ten thousand workers helped to fight the blazes, and eventually the U.S. Army was called in to assist.

Fast-forward nearly forty years to a fire that broke out in Montana. By this time, the United States had installed a fairly effective firefighting organization. So when lightning sparked a fire in Helena National Forest on August 5, 1949, no one suspected that tragedy would strike. Fifteen smoke jumpers and one forest ranger were making their way down into Mann

This 1949 photograph shows the scope of the Mann Gulch fire near Helena, Montana.

39

A cross in Missoula, Montana, commemorates the lives of the twelve smoke jumpers and one forest ranger who perished after a wall of flame raced up a steep hillside during the Mann Gulch blaze in 1949.

Gulch when disaster struck. Sparks threw fire across a ravine and onto the slope where the men were climbing. Fire moves faster uphill than people can run, so the fire quickly overtook most of the firefighters. Ten smoke jumpers and a forest ranger died on the hillside. Two other smoke jumpers died from burns the next day.

Although the number of acres burned by the fire—about 3,000 acres (1,215 ha)—was not as large as many other fires, the deaths caused by the fire were devastating. It was the worst fatality count at that time for wildland firefighters. Many problems contributed to the tragedy. One problem was a lack of communication. The smoke jumpers' radio broke when it fell to the ground, cutting the firefighters off from possibly lifesaving information. The clothing they wore—jeans and cotton shirts—were not fire resistant. The smoke jumpers carried no fireproof shelters.

If any of these things had been different, the firefighters' lives might have been saved. The tragedy taught useful lessons, however. Smoke jumpers now carry much-improved equipment, wear safer clothing, and have more extensive training.

Fires Today

With each disastrous wildland fire, people have looked for lessons to be learned. The fires of 1910 led to the creation of changes in firefighting tactics. The fire at Mann Gulch convinced the firefighting community that their men and women needed to be better prepared and equipped. As the years passed, the number of forest fires seemed to decrease.

However, during the 1970s, the number was once again on the rise. Many experts examining the problem concluded that some fires might in fact be beneficial to forests. Fires help control the accumulation of dead vegetation, which is fuel for more forest fires. With no fires, forests became overgrown and less healthy.

Attitudes toward wildland fires began to change. Perhaps instead of putting out all fires, people argued, some fires should be allowed to burn as long as they didn't threaten the public or natural resources. And maybe rangers could even help the process along by starting controlled fires. It seemed like a good idea until the fire season of 2000.

A Great Loss

In 1994, fourteen firefighters perished on Storm King Mountain in Colorado. Four of them were women. It was the most firefighting personnel to die in a wildland fire since the Big Blowup.

Today, land management professionals agree that keeping forests and parks ecologically healthy can mean letting fires burn or even setting them.

Chapter Five

Fires— Nature's Way

Although wildland fire might seem detrimental to a forest, fires are actually nature's way of clearing and rejuvenating the land. As foresters discovered in the 1970s, forests in which fires had been extinguished rapidly become dense and overgrown. Imagine the number of people it would take to rake up all the leaves that had fallen in the forest during the fall or to chop down all the trees crowding out other plants. Fire can do the job much more efficiently. At the same time, the potential dangers of a prescribed burn, or controlled fire, are always a consideration.

A Healthy Dose of Fire

So fires are nature's way of clearing away dead debris from the forest floor. Then rain washes the burned plant matter away, allowing new plants to grow. Nutrients released from ash into the soil also help new plants grow. The lands that had been burned during the 1988 Yellowstone blaze, for example, were covered with wildflowers the following spring.

Forests not only support plants but animals, too. Although animals can perish from the flames and smoke, most forest animals are able to outrun or hide from a fire. Birds can fly off to another part of the forest. Animals that live underground can remain below the fire until it has passed. When the fire has subsided, the animals quickly return to the forest to feed on the newly sprouting plants and seeds.

Foresters have acknowledged the positive effects that fire can have on forestland. They examine forests for signs of over-

Strong As a Tree

After a forest fire, you might notice some trees still alive. These trees are probably fire resistant. Their bark can withstand the intense heat of a fire. The Douglas fir and longleaf and ponderosa pine can resist surface fires. Forest fires actually help these trees survive, because they clear away other trees that might have shaded them, depriving them of room to grow.

growth, and they determine where fire could benefit the forest. They may then agree that fire would help the forest thrive, and a **prescribed fire** is recommended. That means they have concluded that a fire should be set on purpose.

Managing Fire

The forestry experts who make this decision to burn on purpose are called **fire managers.** By examining the fuel and the

Two firefighters discuss managing a wildfire near the San Bernardino National Forest in southern California. They stand in front of an area that is being burned out.

Officials ignite a prescribed burn in a national park. All prescribed burn projects require a detailed fire plan.

weather conditions, they may prescribe a "management-ignited prescribed fire." This kind of fire is set intentionally and closely monitored by fire personnel. It usually occurs in large forests, where there are no people or buildings nearby.

Fire managers also make decisions about prescribed natural fires, which are fires started by lightning. The managers make the initial decision about whether to allow this type of fire to burn within predetermined guidelines or to put it out. If they allow it to burn, they monitor the fire's progression closely to be sure it doesn't threaten people, homes, or businesses.

The Cerro Grande Fire

Firefighters and fire managers try to control prescribed fires, but fire can be unpredictable. In early May 2000, a prescribed fire was set at Bandelier National Monument, near Los Alamos, New Mexico. Twenty-one fire personnel were on hand to monitor the blaze. The fire seemed to be under control. By the afternoon of the next day, however, the fire could not be tamed. More fire personnel and equipment were needed.

At 1 P.M. on May 5, eighteen hours after the prescribed fire had been started, the fire was declared a wildfire. Unpredicted strong winds and an initial decision by fire managers not to fight the wildfire aggressively led to what would be known as the Cerro Grande fire.

Smoke from the Cerro Grande wildfire fills the sky in early May 2000.

So far, the fire had been contained to the park area. But as the days passed, the fire grew. On May 7, spot fires ignited across a state road. Three days later, on May 10, more than five hundred men and women had been called in to halt the blaze, along with four planes, five air tankers, and twenty-one fire engines. Two days later, on May 12, the eleven thousand residents of Los Alamos were told to evacuate.

A member of a U.S. Forest Service crew walks away from a wall of flames during a wildfire.

Crews from Around the World

The 2000 fire season in the United States drew international help from firefighting teams from Canada, Mexico, New Zealand, and Australia.

By the time the fire ended, some sixteen days after it had been intentionally started, nearly 50,000 acres (20,250 ha) had burned in northern New Mexico and 235 buildings were destroyed. Damage to the city of Los Alamos was estimated to be about $1 billion.

Lessons for the Future

As with all fires, the Cerro Grande prescribed fire offered many lessons for land management teams and firefighters. These experts reviewed what happened in New Mexico to help them improve techniques and decision making for future prescribed fires. And in 2000, the U.S. government agreed to spend more money on national fire control and preparedness.

In 2004, wildland fires in the United States cost more than $500 million to suppress. They burned about 8 million acres (3.2 million ha) and destroyed more than one thousand structures. Determining the best way to control wildland fires—and figuring out how to pay for it—must be a priority.

Another challenge ahead for forestry experts is the successful management of the **wildland-urban interface.** As suburban and semirural populations in many areas of the United States expand into wildland, the danger of fires that threaten people, homes, and businesses as well as wildland also increases. These fires burn in the zone where human development and forested areas meet or coexist. These days, the prevention and management of wildland-urban interface fires should be of great concern to experts and the public alike.

People who work in the forests and fight fires know that although fire is to be feared, it can also be used to our benefit. Fire is a powerful element of nature that should always be appreciated and respected.

Recent Costs and Losses

In the fall of 2003, wildland fires blazed across southern California for several weeks. By the time it was over, 659,902 acres (267,260 ha) had burned and nearly five thousand structures were lost. The fire cost more than $100 million dollars to put out. The greatest loss was of human life—twenty-two people were killed.

Timeline

1825   Fires in Maine and New Brunswick, Canada, burn about 3 million acres (1.2 million ha). The blaze kills 160 people.

1871   The Great Peshtigo Fire burns about 1 million acres (405,000 ha). About 1,300 people die in the fire. The Great Chicago Fire also takes place.

1910   The Big Blowup burns about 3 million acres (1.2 million ha) in Washington, Idaho, and Montana, killing eighty-five people, including seventy firefighters. Ed Pulaski invents the Pulaski firefighting tool.

1940   Smoke jumpers in Nez Perce National Forest in Idaho are enlisted to fight a fire for the first time.

1947   In southern California, helicopters are used for the first time to help fight fires.

1949   A fire at Mann Gulch in Montana's Helena National Forest burns 3,000 acres (1,215 ha) and kills twelve smoke jumpers and one forest ranger.

1988   Fires at Yellowstone National Park burn about 1 million acres (405,000 ha) during a three-month period.

1994   A wildfire on Storm King Mountain in Colorado kills fourteen firefighters.

2000   Cerro Grande, which begins as a prescribed fire, burns about 50,000 acres (20,250 ha) and destroys more than two hundred buildings.

2003	Wildland fires in southern California burn 659,902 acres (267,260 ha), destroy nearly five thousand structures, and kill twenty-two people. Putting the fires out costs more than $100 million dollars.
2004	About 8 million acres (3.2 million ha)—mostly in Alaska—burn in wildland fires in the United States. These fires destroy more than one thousand structures and cost more than $500 million to suppress.

Glossary

blowup—a fire that suddenly increases in speed or intensity, usually causing a change in the firefighting strategy

brush fire—a fire that burns on land covered mainly by shrubs

burning out—setting a fire along the inner edge of a fire line to consume the fuel that is in the path of the main fire

combustible—capable of being burned

creeping fire—a fire that burns with a low flame and spreads slowly

crown fire—a fire that moves through the tops (or crowns) of trees, sometimes independently of the surface fire

ecology—the relationships between living organisms and their environment

fingers of flame—fire that extends from the main body of a fire in long streams, or fingers

fireball—a burst of flame that may appear above a burning tree

fire line—a barrier created by cutting or burning trees so that a fire has no more fuel to consume

fire manager—someone who monitors forests and wildland areas for fire potential, recommends prescribed fires, and determines the plan of action for fires started by lightning

firestorm—a fire accompanied by violent winds

fire triangle—the components needed to start a fire: oxygen, fuel, and heat

fire whirl—a tornado-like funnel of fire that rises from the main fire

flaming front—the part of the fire that burns most rapidly; the fire behind the flaming front is primarily smoldering

flammable—being able to burn; also inflammable

flanks of a fire—the parts of the fire that are roughly parallel to the direction in which the fire is spreading

flare-up—an instance of sudden quickening or strengthening of a fire

forest fire—a fire that burns out of control in forests or woodlands

grass fire—a fire that burns out of control on prairies and fields

ground fire—a fire that burns below the surface in rotting logs and other dead plant material

head of a fire—the part of a fire that moves fastest

helitack crew—firefighters who are transported to a fire by helicopters

hotshot—a dedicated, specially trained wildland firefighter

indraft—a strong wind drawn into a fire by a column of rising air heated by fire

prescribed fire—a fire that is intentionally set, or lightning-caused fire that is allowed to burn in order to reduce the risk of out-of-control wildland fires

project fire—a large fire that requires many resources, firefighting groups, and time to contain

running fire—a fire that is spreading

smoke jumper—a firefighter who jumps from an airplane and parachutes as close as possible to a fire

smoldering fire—a fire that is barely spreading and burns without a flame

snag—a standing dead tree

spot fire—a fire that starts beyond the range of the main fire, caused by flying sparks and embers

surface fire—a fire that burns in fuels lying on or near the ground

wildfire—a fire that burns out of control on open land; forest fires, brush fires, and grass fires are all wildfires

wildland fire—any fire on undeveloped land, including a prescribed fire

wildland-urban interface—the zone where human development and wildland meet or coexist

To Find Out More

Books

Erback, Arlene. *Forest Fires.* Danbury, CT: Children's Press, 1995.

Greenberg, Keith Elliot. *Risky Business: Smokejumper—Firefighter from the Sky.* Woodbridge, CT: Blackbirch Press, 1995.

Lampton, Christopher. *Forest Fire.* Brookfield, CT: Millbrook Press, 1991.

Nobisso, Josephine. *Forest Fires: Run for Your Life!* New York: Mondo Publishing, 2000.

Vogel, Carole G., and Kathryn A. Goldner. *The Great Yellowstone Fire*. San Francisco: Sierra Club Books, 1990.

Videos and DVDs

Fire Wars, PBS NOVA, WGBH Video, 2002.

Smokejumpers: Firefighters from the Sky, Stevan M. Smith, National Smokejumper Association, 2000.

Organizations and Online Sites

Firehouse.com
http://www.firehouse.com
This firefighters' Web site commemorates the fiftieth anniversary of the Mann Gulch fire of 1949 with detailed explanations and pictures.

National Park Service Fire Management Program for Students
http://www.nps.gov/fire/educational/edu_students.html
Geared to students, this U.S. Department of the Interior site includes photographs, interesting facts about fires, a fire quiz, and an explanation of fire as a natural resource.

National Smokejumper Association
http://www.smokejumpers.com
Although the site is aimed at members of the association, you can find out more about the history of smoke jumping and the heroic men and women of this organization.

NOVA Online—Fire Wars
http://www.pbs.org/wgbh/nova/fire/
This site provides detailed information about the NOVA public television program "Fire Wars." You'll find a glossary of fire terms, a look at fire around the world, an explanation of how NOVA was able to film forest fires, and much more.

SmokeyBear.com
http://www.smokeybear.com/wildfires.asp
This site provides safety tips, details about prescribed fires, and mini-case studies with photographs of actual wildfires.

U.S. Department of Agriculture Forest Service
Fire and Aviation Management
http://www.fs.fed.us/fire/
Find out more about the people who battle wildland fires and the U.S. government's fire management strategies, including up-to-date fire maps from the National Interagency Fire Center, which has its own site: *http://www.nifc.gov.*

A Note on Sources

I visited Yellowstone National Park with my husband in 1995 and saw signs of the fires that had ravaged the park in 1988. Driving through the burned part of the forest and seeing the charred remains of the trees eerily poking upward left a deep impression on me. The fires had not snuffed the life out of the park, however. We saw buffalo, moose, and even a lone coyote! When I was asked to write this book, I knew that I wanted to start with the fire at Yellowstone and learn more about it.

Research for this book began at the library. Published references were crucial for obtaining information about the nature of fire and how fires begin. Then I turned my attention to the Internet, focusing my attention on government Web sites. The National Park Service monitors the wildland fires that erupt in our national parks, forests, and monuments. Their Web site has very helpful information about wildland fire education. Linking to other Web sites led me to National

Interagency Fire Center. Here, I found loads of information on fire statistics and fire facts.

It is hard to imagine being able to write a book like this without the aid of the Internet. The organizations listed here were essential for putting together this book. Although I might be able to find information in books about fires, I might not have gotten such detailed information about the Mann Gulch fire, the Big Blowup, smoke jumpers, hotshot and heli-tack crews, and more without the aid of these Web sites. Several of these sites were also ideal for finding information about recent fires that have not yet been written about in book form.

—*Lisa Trumbauer*

Index

Numbers in *italics* indicate illustrations.

About the Author

Lisa Trumbauer is the author of nearly two hundred books for children. The author enjoys researching and writing about any and all topics, and when not traveling or going to Orioles baseball games, she can usually be found at her computer. Trumbauer lives with her husband, Dave, her dog, Blue, and her cats, Cosmo and Cleo, in New Jersey.